INDIE AUTHOR MAGAZINE

HELLO AND WELCOME!

I'm Indie Annie, and I'm thrilled you're reading this gorgeous full-color version of IAM. Did you know that you can also access all the information, education, and inspiration in our app? It's available on both the iOS App Store and Google Play. And for those that prefer to listen to me read articles, you can pop over to Spotify or our website. Happy Reading!

X

IndieAuthorMagazine.com

Download on the App Store

GET IT ON Google Play

Spotify

EMAIL MARKETING

ON THE COVER

INDiE AUTHOR MAGAZINE

PUBLISHER
Chelle Honiker

CREATIVE DIRECTOR
Alice Briggs

CONSULTING EDITOR
Nicole Schroeder

COPY EDITOR
Lisa Thompson

WRITERS
Angela Archer
Elaine Bateman
Patricia Carr
Laurel Decher
Fatima Fayez
Gill Fernley
Greg Fishbone
Remy Flagg
Chrishaun Keller-Hanna
Jac Harmon
Marion Hermannsen

WRITERS
Kasia Lasinska
Bre Lockhart
Anne Lown
Sìne Màiri MacDougall
Merri Maywether
Lasairiona McMaster
Jenn Mitchell
Susan Odev
Clare Sager
Nicole Schroeder
Emilia Zeeland

PUBLISHER
Athenia Creative
6820 Apus Dr.
Sparks, NV, 89436 USA
775.298.1925

ISSN 2768-7880 (online)–ISSN 2768-7872 (print)

From the Publisher

AND JUST LIKE THAT … WE'RE ONE.

I realize that time ceased to have meaning when the world went topsy-turvy. What used to be a minute started to feel like seven hours. And what used to feel like a month sometimes felt like a single minute.

It's like we all collectively jumped in a Tardis and started cranking the knobs.

With that in mind, I was still gobsmacked to see a major milestone on my calendar. *Indie Author Magazine* is officially one year old.

To put it in perspective, that equates to:

- 86,000+ reads
- 253 articles
- 160,000+ words
- 11,000+ social media likes

… And one grateful team. Thank you for your support, and I hope that you'll continue to let us help you reach your author-business goals.

We have exciting new projects in the works for our second year, starting with an Author Tech Summit in July, expanded video interviews on our YouTube Channel, an advisory board made up of smart industry insiders, and an in-person mastermind in San Antonio, Texas.

We're just getting started.

On a personal note, I became a grandmother on April 4, 2022, as my daughter Kelsea and her husband Kevin welcomed a healthy, beautiful daughter, Elowyn Madeline Adams. I'm a thrilled "Mimi," and my new favorite pastime is spamming the team Slack channel with photos.

Thank you for a fantastic first year. Here's to many more.

To Your Success,
Chelle
Publisher
Indie Author Magazine

Attitude of Top Indies

I work with self-published authors across the entire spectrum of success, but the main thing I see from those who head to five figures a month and beyond is confident persistence. They will do what it takes, without compromising their principles. They write what they like, but with an eye toward what the readers want to read. It's an overlap of what brings both the author and the reader satisfaction.

A great story delivered to the right readership. Repeat that and win.

For those who write passion projects, temper your expectations. If you write with the audience in mind, you'll better deliver what they are looking for, and they will respond better than having a questionable story foisted upon them.

The book has to be good enough, a great story or a good story told in a great way. It happens when the author is a critical reader. High-performing authors see what resonates, recognize the ebbs and flows of a well-paced tale. They deliver a story that people enjoy reading.

A great story can get you to ten thousand dollars in a month but putting that book into the broader readership of the genre is what keeps the high-performing indies accelerating to ever increasing levels of income.

High performers don't have to love the marketing side, but they do understand it. They undertake marketing as a series of tasks. They are on the outside of the story, showing the title to those who will be interested. It's not "buy my book," but "this is a story that will entertain you, similar to others that you like but unique."

The seven-figure authors embrace the marketing side every bit as much as the artistic side. And that leads to rarified air, those unicorns who are at the top of the game. But you don't have to go there to have a lucrative career.

Write a great story with the audience of that genre in mind and then put it into their hands. That is the secret of high-performing indies. There are a lot of steps to get there, but none of them are insurmountable. ■

Craig Martelle

AUTHOR·TECH·SUMMIT

Summer, 2022
AuthorTechSummit.com

What the Indie Author Can Learn from the Sanderson Kickstarter

> **He makes you want to be part of it.**

My dear friends greeted me at the door of their home, sat me down, placed a tablet in my hands, and pressed play. I got the e-book *A Year of Sanderson*.

Bill, my husband, saw it later that night. He rolled his eyes at Sanderson's heart-wrenching words of regret and declared that he wrote another book. That was no surprise to him. He did not see the other three coming. He got the hardback collection.

In early March 2022, Sci-Fi and Fantasy author Brandon Sanderson's "Surprise! Four Secret Novels" Kickstarter campaign shocked authors and those outside the industry alike, including Bill and me. Within just seventy-two hours of publication, Sanderson's campaign surpassed twenty million dollars, becoming the highest-funded Kickstarter project of all time and drawing attention from media organizations such as CNBC, Slate Magazine, and even Kickstarter itself. Even as I'm writing this article, the campaign total continues to climb rapidly as does its popularity.

As a fan, this experience was engaging and thrilling. Sanderson had his entire script in his head and delivered it with the glee of a man who *loves* what he does for a living and telling you all the great things about it in equal measure. He makes you want to be part of it.

As an author and artist with three successful Kickstarter book and merchandise box campaigns under my belt, this experience was validating and exciting. Kickstarter campaigns

> **"Kickstarter campaigns have been a rewarding way to recoup my production costs for both the book and the merch boxes."**

have been a rewarding way to recoup my production costs for both the book and the merch boxes, including royalties for my co-authors. It even provides a tidy profit to put toward ads, promos, or the next project.

THE SANDERSON KICKSTARTER CAN TEACH US SEVERAL THINGS.

I can talk about this all day, but I don't like talking alone, and after observing a recent Kickstarter cohort led by Russell Nohelty and Monica Leonelle, authors of *Get Your Book Selling on Kickstarter,* I decided to reach out to Nohelty and get his thoughts.

"YOU MAKE WAY MORE MONEY WITH WAY FEWER PEOPLE."

"This is the big thing about Kickstarter that I'm always talking about," Nohelty says, "and I think that it's finally getting through. You make way more money with way fewer people.

"[Sanderson's Kickstarter backers] are a fraction of a fraction of a fraction of the audience who buys his books," he says. "His books sell literally millions of copies, and yet with just fifty-six thousand people, he was able to raise five times his normal advance in one day."

Since Nohelty and I spoke, the Sanderson campaign has raised a total of twenty-nine million dollars with 129,000 backers. That's a huge number of backers, but it still reflects 1 percent of his audience that purchased his book. He won't have that same amount

> **[Sanderson's Kickstarter backers] are a fraction of a fraction of a fraction of the audience who buys his books.**
> **- Russell Nohelty**

after fees and production costs, but he will have far more than his advance—roughly 2.5 million per book—in a much shorter time from a relatively tiny number of people, people who paid that much to be part of this experience.

This tracks when I run the numbers on my campaigns. My campaigns are in the $2,600 range funded by an average of fifty backers. I tend to keep my mailing list lean, and it's my main audience when I talk about my campaigns. So when I looked at the totals, I was shocked to see that I was running just under 2 percent of my mailing list.

Nohelty, on the other hand, has twenty-plus successful publishing Kickstarters, raising over three hundred thousand dollars on the platform for novels, comics, anthologies, nonfiction, and audio dramas.

According to his Kickstarter data, even though the number of backers on his campaigns varies from just under thirty to over a thousand, he averages 385 backers per campaign, roughly 1 percent of his active list.

Kickstarter, more than any other platform, helps you identify and connect with your superfans. Fans will purchase anything you release because they enjoy you and your work and they feel part of it. And because they are so invested, they're also willing to spend a premium for first access—Kickstarters usually offer rewards months before they're available to the public—as well as exclusives only available with the campaign, fun merch, and even a chance to become a character in your work.

Yes, superfans are willing to pay a premium, but how much of one? More than you would expect. The most popular pledge on

> **Yes, superfans are willing to pay a premium, but how much of one? More than you would expect.**

Kickstarter is twenty-five dollars, which is already much higher than the royalty of a single book on Amazon, but the average pledge for all campaigns was eighty-eight dollars while a fully funded campaign averaged ninety-six dollars.

What's the difference between a fully funded campaign and one that misses the mark?

YOUR FOLLOWING IS KEY.

According to Crowdfunding Statistics (2021): Market Size and Growth (https://fundera.com/resources/crowdfunding-statistics), crowdfunding projects average forty-seven backers. Fully funded crowdfunding projects have an average of three hundred backers. As we saw above, the pledge difference is minimal. The number of backers combined with a reasonable goal—Nohelty recommends five hundred dollars for a novel campaign—is the key.

Wade Peterson agrees. The award-winning Science Fiction and Fantasy author recently launched a Kickstarter for a special edition of his book, *Badlands Born*. I asked what he gained from doing a Kickstarter rather than a traditional launch.

"For me, it was about finding an audience and discoverability for a book that didn't fit neatly into a genre niche," he says. "My series strategy is still more about building an audience than it is about chasing sales, and Kickstarter seemed to be a better bet for finding my niche than spending the same amount of time and/or effort on Facebook or Amazon ads."

> **"**
> **It was about finding an audience and discoverability for a book that didn't fit neatly into a genre niche.**
> **-Wade Peterson**
> **"**

Many authors who write books that can't be immediately defined by genre find that Kickstarter is a great way to not only find their superfans but generate enough income to go into their traditional launch in the black.

This worked for J.R. Frontera, whose western Sci-Fi pulp adventure *Bargain at Bravebank* earned 800 percent over her goal.

"I want to really engage with my superfans and the readers that I do have because I would prefer to have people that really enjoy my books—a smaller group of very good quality readers versus a massive group of people that will forget me tomorrow. This was by design, and I operate on that basis." She says her best one-day sale was $150. The first day of her Kickstarter, she earned $1,100.

"I was getting too frustrated because I felt that there were too many variables outside of my control—working with all the retailers, working with Facebook and Amazon ads. There's a lot of things you have no control over. I can spend all of my time worrying about that stuff, trying to control things I can't control, or I can focus on delivering a quality book and a quality package. I can spend time figuring out where my ideal readers are, go there, have a good time with them, and introduce them to my books, and then I'm happy because my readers are happy."

Running a Kickstarter campaign is not a get-rich-quick scheme or a full-time living. It's a launch that takes planning, knowing what your readers want, and communicating it often and well. It's a platform that allows you to find the audience that will help you keep making the books you want to make instead of bending your vision to the market. ◼

Chrishaun Keller-Hanna

Dear Indie Annie,

I've been criticized by teachers and even friends and family for my poor grammar. I know it's bad, but does that mean I should give up writing anything at all?

Grammarless in Gravelotte

DEAR GRAMMARLESS,

Let's start by changing your name, my sweet child. How about … Grammarfree?

Think of grammar as you would the rules of the road, or as my friends in the UK would say, the Highway Code. These rules or codes provide guidelines that navigate road users safely to their destinations. Rules differ from state to state and country to country, as do the potential penalties for ignoring them. Throughout history, they have changed and adapted to new technology.

At one time, a man with a red flag had to walk in front of an automobile to warn other road users of its approach—not a sight we see very often today.

That said, some believe these codes of behavior are hard and fast rules and it is a criminal act of extreme negligence to break them. However, we all know of parts of the world where there appear to be no rules of the road, and, for the most part, drivers, passengers, and pedestrians get to where they are going safely.

Need help from your favorite Indie Aunt?
Ask Dear Indie Annie a question at
IndieAnnie@indieauthormagazine.com

Does that mean that one should drive recklessly through town without paying attention to our neighbors? No, of course, it doesn't, my dear.

It does mean, though, that you should think again about what it means to be a writer.

Are you a conduit for a series of words funneled through a collection of transitory grammar rules? Or are you a creator of worlds, the teller of tales?

I would argue, dear one, that you are the latter and that is what makes you a writer.

I am not saying that grammar is not important. I once rode behind the driver on a purple Harley-Davidson around Marrakech and would have given away my firstborn for some road signs. But what a thrilling ride!

When you write a great story, you take your readers on a journey. Many will argue that if the story pulls them in enough, they will ignore the small grammatical bumps in the road. It is the story that counts. You are a storyteller first and foremost.

Happy writing,
Indie Annie

10 TIPS FOR
EMAIL SUBJECT LINES

Aside from writing and publishing a new book, email marketing is often touted as the key to many authors' success. Whether you send regular emails weekly or monthly or use list-building tactics like newsletter swaps, group promos, and reader magnets, there's little point in spending all that time creating great content if it's not getting opened.

Your readers' email inboxes are bursting at the seams with marketers vying for their attention. Learning how to write solid, enticing email subject lines that entice your readers is a skill, but these tips will help.

1 MAKE THE SUBJECT LINE REDUNDANT

Email inboxes remain a personal space, so the focus of your emails shouldn't always be about sales. It's about playing the long game and building relationships. Show your personality, give glimpses of backstory, and make your emails entertaining enough so that your readers feel as if they know you. Then when your email pops up in their inbox, they'll see your name and click—because they know they're getting an entertaining email from a friend.

Pro Tip: A great place to start building this relationship is by nailing your welcome sequence with a minimum of three to five emails. Plot it out just like you would a book: Follow the hero's journey, or go for a basic beginning, middle, and end. Don't forget to add a call to action at the end of each email.

2 GIVE THEM A HEADS-UP

Many people, when faced with something new—e.g., signing up to your email—feel uncertain or distrustful, which will lead them to reject your offer.

You can help avoid this rejection by letting them know what to look for. Let's say you're doing a group promo in BookFunnel and someone clicks to download your reader magnet. Telling them to look out for an email from you with a specific subject line can help them overcome doubts, hesitations, and inaction.

(3) BE LESS FORGETTABLE

We're so used to seeing certain words or phrases, they tend to lose their visual impact. Try the following tactics to catch your readers' eye:

- Use numbers
- Use square brackets
- Use hashtags
- Use emoji
- Say it differently

Square brackets stand out, and they can be great for drawing attention to part of the subject line. For example: [WARNING] This email contains peril.

Get creative with your copywriting and use unusual words or phrases. Say it differently, and you'll have a better chance of standing out.

---

(4) LESS IS OFTEN MORE

With more users viewing emails on mobile devices, the amount of visible text for subject lines needs to be considered.

Devices vary in how many characters are shown in the subject line, but aiming for around thirty characters should stand you in good stead. It's short, but this is where using the pre-header text function comes in handy.

Pre-header, meta, or preview text, as it's interchangeably called, is the little bit of preview text that appears after your subject line and should be around fifty characters. This offers another opportunity to stoke your reader's interest. Each email service provider is different, so check their help pages to find out how to add yours.

---

(5) QUICK! CREATE URGENCY

Creating a sense of urgency is one of the oldest tricks in the sales book for the simple reason that people *hate* to feel as if they're missing out.

Inertia and procrastination are a default setting for many, and when given the choice, they'll always choose to put off decisions until later—unless it's urgent and they feel they'll be left behind.

Pro Tip: Apply urgency in a creative yet authentic way. Using scarcity and urgency is an easy way to boost open rates, but don't rely on them too often. Only use them when there's a genuine call for immediate action. Otherwise, people will learn to hold back and wait until your next sale.

6 EVOKE A SENSE OF THINGAMY

Did you spot that subheading? Did you wonder what a "thingamy" is? It could have just said "Evoke a sense of curiosity," but instead, this idea combines tip #3 with this tip to create an open loop. As humans, we have an innate desire for closure, so using mystery in your subject line creates an unanswered question (an open loop) in the readers' minds—which triggers a strong urge to fill that gap.

"SHOCKER: I can't believe she said THIS" works as a subject line because we can't resist not knowing who and what the person said.

Pro Tip: Leverage curiosity in different ways by adding specificity. For example, "Before you read another book, read this" or "Before you go to bed at night, don't do this." Tie the action to what they regularly do to really catch their attention.

7 DON'T BE AFRAID TO BE A LITTLE RISQUE

If you're not afraid to push the envelope, be a little more controversial. In a world where being authentic and showing our personalities is more the norm, sometimes it actually helps to use controversy to polarize your audience because so often, polarity creates popularity.

Try something like "[genre] readers are the worst for this…" By combining a risque statement with curiosity, people won't be able to help opening the email to find out more.

While controversy is powerful, it does depend on the audience. You need to make it relevant and have some credibility to back it up. Do make sure to answer the question in the email so they don't feel like they were tricked into clicking.

Pro Tip: If you pose a question or make a strong statement in your email subject line, then you need to make sure that your email content answers it, or people will see your emails as clickbait, and you'll lose credibility.

8 KEEP IT CASUAL, DAVE

Some of the most effective email subject lines are casual and feel personal. They read like emails you might receive from a friend. Connecting with your readers on an emotional level is one of the best ways to engage with them.

According to Klaviyo (https://klaviyo.com), a business marketing organization, addressing subscribers by their first names in the subject line can boost open rates 60 percent of the time. Another method to create emotional resonance in your subject lines is to speak to your reader's hopes, fantasies, and dreams through future pacing. In other words, help your audience visualize what could be possible in the near future in just a few words.

For example:

- Unleash your inner James Bond
- Imagine yourself one year from today, Alex…
- Erika, wanna write emails that actually get opened?

9 HERE'S TIP NUMBER NINE: KEEP IT PRACTICAL

This is a practical subject line. Just tell them exactly what's in the email: "Download your e-book here," "7 reasons to unsubscribe from …," "Your ARC copy link is enclosed." The promise is clear, and they know what they're getting when they open. This type of subject line is great if you're sending them a reader magnet or freebie. Just cut to the chase, and in that way, you build credibility and trust—which are essential to a good reader experience.

Pro Tip: Some words are red flags for spam filters, such as "free," "discount," "100% off," and "apply now." Email service provider Active Campaign has a handy article about how to stay out of spam filters (https://activecampaign.com/blog/spam-words).

10 HAVE A COMPETITION–WITH YOURSELF

You won't be able to cram all these tips in one subject line, so come up with some variations for each campaign and go with the one that gives you the strongest emotional reaction. Then pick a runner-up and A/B split test—if it's within your email service provider package. If not, run with the first subject line to your whole list and use the second subject line to resend the email to the people who didn't open the first one.

The goal is to work out the best types of subject line for the type of message you're sending and which ones resonate with your audience. Adopt a curiosity mindset rather than viewing it as another task that takes you away from writing because it'll pay off in the long-term—like when you have a new release or you're pushing a promotion.

Pro Tip: Remember, it's not the job of the email to do the actual selling. The main job of your email is to build a relationship and get people to move further down the buyer's funnel toward the point of sale. ◾

Angela Archer

ROBYN WIDEMAN'S
AUDIENCE-FIRST APPROACH TO PUBLISHING

One of the many things I admire about the indie author community is how they are of the mindset that there is enough pie for all of us. Because of this, when an indie author has information that can assist another author, they step in and share it. One of those helpful people is Robyn Wideman.

Before I get ahead of myself, let me introduce Robyn. He writes teen High Fantasy, LitRPG, and GameLit, all with elements of Science Fiction. In addition to being an author, he is a publisher under his Magicblood Media brand.

The first time I met Robyn, we were at a pre-pandemic conference/writers retreat. A group of roughly 150 authors was holed away for six days. We had two days to build friendships that endured distance. When we weren't talking about our real worlds, we added words to our fictional ones. Then came two days of learning about the business, followed by two days of writing. At this point, the group of authors was friends. We wrote a little and talked a lot about how to apply what we learned at the conference.

In one of these collaborative learning sessions, I was lucky enough to have Robyn explain how to read reports and use the information. It was just enough

information to apply the newfound knowledge, knowing there was more to learn. Thankfully, three years later, Robyn was willing to answer the questions I didn't know to ask and answered them from the perspective of his role as a publisher.

THE BEGINNINGS OF ROBYN'S AUTHOR JOURNEY

Before Facebook groups, indie authors and aspiring authors discussed the market on Amazon Kindle's KBoards. Robyn spent his time there learning all he could about the publishing industry. "The hard lessons that usually come from experience, I learned for free from authors who shared what they knew." They taught him about promo launches and the importance of blurbs, covers, and keywords. When he had a grasp on how to be a successful indie author, he tested the waters.

On April 15, 2015, he published a couple of shorter stories. After the stories proved that Robyn had a viable product, he published *The Son of Soron* and *The Missing Mage*. The rapid release launch of the two coming-of-age Fantasies took place days after each other, holding control over a promise Robyn made to himself. When he reached fifty dollars a day in sales, he'd quit one of his two day jobs because that meant his writing was working. Within a week, the sales surpassed his goal. Then he set another benchmark to help him decide which job to leave. Once again, he went above and beyond what he set. Within a month of his launch, Robyn quit both jobs. Both titles are still in the top 100 of their categories today.

WHAT DOES WRITING LOOK LIKE AS A PUBLISHER?

As a publisher, Robyn helps his authors maintain the structure while allowing authors to explore their creativity. His feedback for ideas is always based on whether the publishing company could sell it.

Using a philosophy of "It is way easier to write a book to an audience than it is to find an audience for your book," Robyn uses metadata to determine if a book will sell. For example, when someone approaches him with a story, his first question is, "What are the keywords?" When an author can give that information, they prove there is an audience for the story they want to tell.

AS A PUBLISHER, DO YOU WORK MORE AS A PLOTTER OR PANTSER?

Robyn prefers writing within a hybrid organization system. He starts the story with a plotline and lets the story grow from there. "When writing a Fantasy series, an organized plotline keeps the story consistent," Robyn says. Otherwise, the author could end up in a situation where the character uses one spell type in one book and a different spell in a subsequent book in the series. "Keeping an up-to-date spreadsheet is critical to making writing in series not a brain buster."

In other words, a semblance of an outline is necessary. "However," Robyn added, "with that being said, if someone comes up with a cool idea that doesn't fit with the outline, I'll make the outline fit the cool idea. As an author, we have to know when to pivot. Authors are organic creators. Even as they are typing the story, new ideas are flowing."

IS NAVIGATING THE MARKET AS A PUBLISHER DIFFERENT THAN AS A WRITER?

Robyn's passion, especially as a publisher, is metadata. This was the add-on to what he was trying to explain to me all those years ago. He also explained that metadata is necessary because readers aren't looking for authors until they are familiar with their work. They're looking for a certain type of book. "The metadata presents your story in a way that says my book is what you're looking for."

We have control over the metadata on the Amazon dashboard. "The seven keywords are what Amazon uses to put your book in front of the

reader. It will do more for you than spending money on ads. You can find the ones to use in Publisher Rocket." He added that authors can also use the search bar on Amazon. "You can type the first terms. After that, Amazon will supply options by auto-filling with suggestions. The algorithm predicts what you're looking for."

This method also applies to market research for writing. As a publisher, Robyn is interested in the stories people are looking for. He searches for keywords, character types, and tropes. In particular, he looks at how many people are searching for that information and how many authors are writing to meet the need. Through the research, he can piece together what story readers want.

After the aha moments, he explained the process using terms we've heard. "People call it 'write to market.' I call it finding out if there is an audience for the story."

HOW DO YOU LOOK AT FORMATTING?

As far as formatting is concerned, it is one of the simplest aspects of publishing. Within its site, Amazon offers help for the author with the finished product. He explained that formatting an e-book is roughly a thirty-second process. Paperbacks require a little more attention to different details like margins. "And there are lots of great software options like Vellum and Atticus that make formatting paperbacks much easier," Robyn says.

What confuses those new to indie publishing is that books are art. This is why, where formatting is concerned, many standards are tied to preferences. So different authors ascribe to different methods. "For instance, some will use italics when a character communicates telepathically while others use dialogue tags. There is no rule." With that said, Robyn recommends reviewing tables and images on different devices before publishing, especially with e-readers. On one device, the image meant to enhance the reading experience can interfere with the reader's ability to read clearly because it covers the text or isn't fully on the screen.

He closed the topic, reiterating that new authors should visit the help pages on Amazon. "They have great resources for formatting."

HOW CAN AN AUTHOR PROVIDE READERS EXTRA VALUE?

"Extra value is inconsequential if the reader is getting value," Robyn says. "The end result is the same if, when they put the book down, they're super excited for the next book and are looking for it already. If I've created a world that they're excited about and want to read, I've given them something they value. I'm not looking to give extra value. I'm looking to give the reader something they really want."

He continues, "I think you're better off writing the best book you can and selling it to as many people as you can. There's no extra in that. It's literally all or nothing."

WHAT DOES SUCCESS MEAN TO YOU?

"As an author, writing something that my readers will enjoy," Robyn says. "As a publisher, my success comes when I'm able to sell that story and get high rankings, especially when I'm working with other authors."

The conversation slowed to favorite reads, movies, and hopes for the future. Even then, like the authors who helped him years ago, Robyn was forthcoming with information that would help authors new and experienced. He said, "Here's a little tip. Whatever is hot on TV will sell in books too." People will see a movie or a great television program and want to extend the experience. They can do this with books we write with the help of metadata.

I had to chuckle because he is an intuitive publisher, and looking at the tip from the perspective of a rabid reader, I knew he was right. ■

Merri Maywether

Spring Clean Your Email List

YOUR GUIDE TO REMOVING BOTS, DEAD ADDRESSES, AND NON-RESPONDERS

You've likely heard that building your email list is an important part of marketing your books. If you have a large list of raving, highly engaged fans who can't wait to read your next book, then you have a great chance of selling lots of copies of your new release with just a few simple emails.

In addition to building your email list, you also need to keep it clean. This is also known as improving your list hygiene or improving your email list health. But before you get out the Clorox and the rubber gloves, it's important to understand why these steps are so important in the first place.

WHY KEEP YOUR EMAIL LIST CLEAN?

Cleaning your list is simply getting rid of any bad addresses on your list, along with anyone who hasn't opened any of your emails in the last ninety days.

There are three main reasons to cull these addresses from your list:

1. If you're emailing people who don't read them, you may be paying more for your email program than you need to. Cleaning up your list of people who will never open your emails gives you room for more of those raving fans we mentioned without paying extra to go up to the next tier on your email provider subscription.

2. If the majority of the people on your list are genuinely engaged subscribers, then your click-through rates and other statistics will be more accurate. If your list is full of fake addresses or people who never open an email, your stats will be skewed. You won't easily be able to tell which content is attracting your audience and what's genuinely not working for them.

3. Emailing bad addresses can damage your reputation with your service provider. This can potentially get you a warning from your provider, get your account frozen, or result in sending more of your perfectly innocent emails into spam folders.

Bad addresses can include any number of faulty or fake email addresses.

Spam traps are addresses set up by internet service providers and blacklist providers to catch spammers and block their emails.

Malicious opt-ins happen because a person or bot keeps filling in your opt-in form with real email addresses from people who haven't given you permission to email them. You can sometimes spot these as bots tend to use random numbers and letters for the username, but it's not always that easy. In this case, you're likely to get a higher number of spam complaints from people who didn't sign up to receive your emails.

Invalid email addresses might be misspelled genuine addresses, older addresses that are no longer in use, or addresses with a problem, such as a missing @ symbol. These addresses will never work, and they'll show up in your statistics as bounced emails. Some email providers will review your account if your bounce rate goes over 5 percent, so this does matter.

Bot addresses are read only by a computer and never a real human. While they won't add to your bounce rate, they may forward your email to other email addresses that weren't signed up to your list.

Anybody who didn't sign up to your list is also considered a bad address. Don't add people to your mailing list if they haven't expressly asked you to or opted in on one of your forms. It's really bad form and hurts your reputation—and, depending on where you live and the terms of service with your email provider, it could even be illegal.

WHAT TO DO BEFORE YOU CLEAN YOUR LIST

Before you embark on any major newsletter spring cleaning, familiarize yourself with your email list and your statistics. Review a few months and check your average stats. Keep an eye on these figures, partly because you want to know that what you're sending is what people want to read but also because if you're getting lower-than-usual open and click-through rates, along with more unsubscribes and spam complaints, it might be time to clean up your list.

Next, take a look at the emails on your bounce list in your email provider dashboard. Any hard bounces are addresses that won't work, and these will be automatically cleaned by your software. Open your list of soft bounces as you may be able to rescue some of these. You'll be able to see if they're missing an @ symbol or have some other error, and you can edit the address to fix it. You might also see some addresses

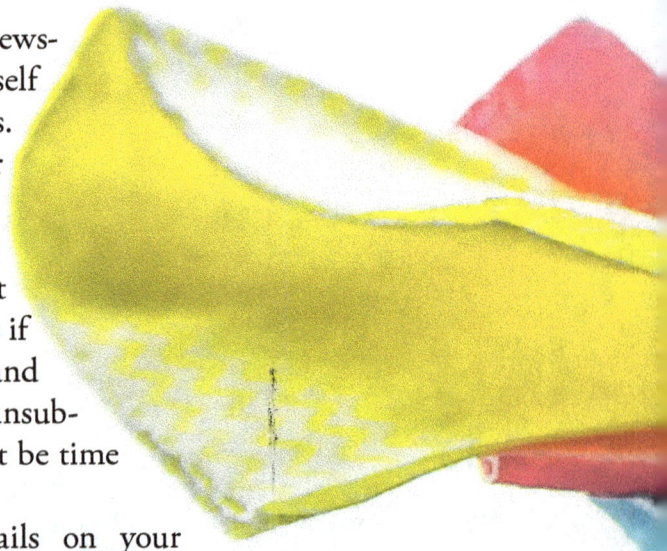

that have obvious spelling errors, such as fred@hotamil.com or maryb@gmial.cmo. Again, just edit, and you're good to go.

You can try one more thing before you clean your list. It's worth a final attempt to re-engage your subscribers who don't open your emails anymore or click any of your links before you delete them for good. If you can convince them to engage with you again, then congrats, you've just upped your open rate and can maybe start to change these people into the raving fans you really want on your list.

We can't give you a step-by-step guide here as we can't cover every email software out there, but you should be able to get a list of your inactive subscribers. Next, segment your list so that you're only sending an email to these subscribers. Think about what will motivate them to come back. Can you offer a special discount or a code? Would a competition entry or a free story work? You know your readers best, so take the time to chew this over. You can also do this with an automated sequence if your software has that option. You can set up a sequence that will automatically send a re-engagement email after so many days of not opening your emails.

You can then move on to cleaning your list.

HOW TO IMPROVE YOUR LIST HYGIENE AND INCREASE YOUR STATS

You can clean your list in several ways:

1. Manually

Go through your email list and manually remove any bouncing emails you can't fix. Delete any inactive subscribers and check your list for any obviously fake addresses. Delete any duplicate email addresses.

It's time-consuming and not the most fun you'll ever have in your life, but it works.

2. Set up automations

Depending on the software you have and your subscription level, you may have automation options. If so, you can set up sequences to automatically remove inactive subscribers after a set number of days. You can tell your software what to look for and have it do the hard work for you.

3. Use an email scrubbing service

A quick Google search will bring you a variety of services that will clean your email list for you. With some services, you'll have to import your subscriber list as a CSV file and then import it back into your email software after it has been cleaned. Others will integrate with some of the main email providers for a more automatic clean.

Once your email list is clean, aim to keep it that way with regular maintenance, and your reputation will be safe. You'll know what content is working for your subscribers, what they want more of, and what they aren't interested in.

All done. You can put the rubber gloves away now. ■

Gill Fernley

JPG VS. TXT

ARE NEWSLETTERS BETTER WHEN THEY INCLUDE IMAGES?

L oads of articles compare the pros and cons of images or plain text in email newsletters.

Let's cut to the chase: They both have their pros and cons. Chances are also good that no single article will sway you one way or the other if you're fixed in your ways and you have your reasons for plain text or images.

Since that's probably the case, let's see how we can use plain text and images more effectively and efficiently.

IMAGES

If an image is worth a thousand words, couldn't we just insert one image in our newsletter and call it a day?

Well, technically, yes. (Although email spam filters really don't like emails with no text.) But we are writers, after all! Ideally, a balance of text and images can pack the most punch. Let's first look at how images can help us connect with our audience.

PROS

- **A Thousand Words:** If those who are only going to skim your newsletter aren't going to read a thousand words and one image is worth a thousand words, well, you get the math.
- **Beauty:** You can describe your dog (or your book's hero) all day, but a simple photo will do all that for you.
- **Brand:** A well-chosen photo can elevate your brand though it's important to keep in mind how often *personal* can be more important than *professional*.

CONS

- **Blocked:** In older browsers or computers, images might be blocked from emails. Newer technology might see images as a place to hide viruses.
- **File Size:** This is so 1999, but if you don't resize and optimize your images and actually do send that 4-megabyte behemoth from your fancy phone, it will weigh down certain email providers (and just annoy people) with slower loading times.

This is a gorgeous photo of a dog in a red bow with a stunning gray backdrop.

Yes, it's cute. Yes, it's professional.

But could it be too cute? Too professional? Staged? Studio? Unless you have pro lighting in your office, no one would believe this was really the newsletter author's dog.

So what would it do for the email? If it's not the author's dog or otherwise has nothing to do with the author's work, stories, or characters, then it's just another cute dog picture.

On the other hand, consider a candid photo of the author's dog and a deer.

Already, the connection between the author and the reader is deeper. This is the author's dog. No backdrop, no professional lighting, no studio.

Pair the image with the right story, and that connection can grow even stronger. Perhaps the author explains how the deer represents the author's recently deceased mother, who whispered to the author in his meditation that she would appear "in an unexpected form" and that he should be on the lookout for her.

At this point, hopefully, the reader is saying, "Forget the blue backdrop and pro lighting! Tell me more about the deer and the dog and the spirits."

See how easily one photo can be "pretty" but not have a story, but another, more personal photo can pack in so much story?

Studies like the jam experiment performed by psychologists Sheena Iyengar and Mark Lepper in 2000 have shown how people react when given too many choices. Give shoppers six choices of jam, and you'll have more sales and more satisfied customers. But give them twenty-four different kinds of jam, and they are overwhelmed. They can't decide (because they actually have too many choices).

Help your reader "choose" what to focus on. Don't overwhelm them with photos. Use just one, and then give it a caption or a story.

The question then becomes not so much if you should use images in your newsletters but which images you should use and why.

PLAIN TEXT

As boring and old school as it may seem, plain text newsletters still have a lot going for them.

PROS

- **It Works:** Even on old browsers and ancient phones, your newsletter will work. Spam filters prefer it too.
- **Accessibility:** Plain text newsletters (or those that include image descriptions or alt text for their images) are accessible for people who are blind or visually disabled and use a screen reader.
- **Preference:** Some people just like it. Plain and simple.
- **Focus:** Plain text has no graphics or pretty photo distractions. Just words. Get to the point.
- **Personal:** The original rationale behind text-only emails was that they seemed more like a personal note to a friend (as opposed to a marketing pitch from a company).

CONS

- **Boring:** There is no color, graphics, and sometimes not even an embedded link.
- **Limited:** Sure, you could write a paragraph about how beautiful the sunset is … or you could share a photo.
- **Focus:** Images can help the reader focus if there's too much text.

The discussion about images or plain text evolves into how to most effectively use each one.

For example, if this paragraph just goes and goes and goes and doesn't have any punctuation—well, maybe a comma here and there—the message, and your readers, can get lost. Unlike in a printed newspaper, where the layout of the width of the columns is set, reading digital text will then be dependent on the device or screen or resolution of the screen. If you're reading this on a phone, this paragraph is likely filling up the entire screen by now. It doesn't really flow, right? It all gets jumbled up. What if you had something important to say at this point? How would you, while limited to plain text, be able to emphasize it?

A.

Breath.

Of.

Fresh.

Air.

Now, let's continue with a few more sentences here that will grow into a paragraph that "frames" those five lines above. Now your eyes are focused on what's above, and you might even go back there and read it again.

Purely visually, let's see how that compares to those same five words in a single sentence. Ready?

A. Breath. Of. Fresh. Air.

Or without the periods:

A breath of fresh air.

See how much emphasis we can have by using the minimal tools at our plain text disposal? Remember that when writing for a digital audience (which is, of course, most of the entire planet), we, the authors, can only do so much with the formatting of our words on the page.

Now think of your email newsletter. What if the main message was *A Breath of Fresh Air*? If the readers scanned your email quickly and only got those five words (a breath of fresh air), that could be considered a successful newsletter.

Think of dialogue in a fiction novel. Reading dialogue not only *seems* like it reads faster, it actually *does* read faster. Shorter paragraphs and more white space leads to a clarity and peace of mind that adds to the ease (and pleasure) of reading for the audience.

AND JUST FOR FUN ... PLAIN TEXT ART

Although we've covered the limitations of plain text, let's take a look at what some very creative plain text artists have come up with.

Plain Text Art:

```
$$$$$$$$$$$$$$$$$$$$$$$$$$$$$
$$$$$$$$$$$$$$$$$$$$$$$$$$$$$$
$$$$$'`$$$$$$$$$$$$$$'`$$$
$$$$$$  $$$$$$$$$$$$$  $$$$
$$$$$$$  '$/ `/ `$' .$$$$
$$$$$$$$. i  i  /! .$$$$$
$$$$$$$$$.--'--'   $$$$$$
$$^^$$$$$'        J$$$$$$
$$$   ~""   `.   .$$$$$$$
$$$$$e,       ;  .$$$$$$$$
$$$$$$$$$$$$.'   $$$$$$$$$
$$$$$$$$$$$$$.   $$$$$$$$
$$$$$$$$$$$$$$    $by&TL$
```

From <u>Christopher Johnson's ASCII Art Collection</u>. ◼

Bradley Charbonneau

Choosing an ESP— No Sixth Sense Required!

THE INS AND OUTS OF EMAIL SERVICE PROVIDERS

Congratulations! You've poured your heart and soul onto the page, and your book has come to life. You've planned the launch to end all launches and even built the perfect landing page where your legion of fans can subscribe to your newsletter while they anxiously wait, cash in hand, for your next release.

Sounds like every author's dream, right? Well, of course, it does. It's how we all hope and pray our launches will go, but there's one minor detail you have to attend to yet, and getting it right can overwhelm even the most seasoned authors.

You can have the most successful launch in all of indie author history, but it won't help your long-term strategy if you can't collect your reader's contact information and use it in a way that's relevant to your author business. That's where email service providers (ESP) come in.

An ESP is a company that provides the technology platform or service that collects and manages email subscriber lists. Their services range from simple contact information collection to marketing campaigns, beta reader management, and even sophisticated data analytics.

If all ESPs were the same, it wouldn't matter which you chose. While most provide a similar set of basic features, they can vary greatly when it comes to the tools that help an author manage their subscriber list.

Fortunately, you don't need to have ESP to choose an ESP. Most of us start the decision-making process by asking our author friends, scouring through posts in networking groups, or searching the web for reviews. These are all suitable places to begin, but going these routes often presents another set of challenges that can lead to confusion and frustration.

Turning to the web can point you to some really helpful information, but it can also send you down a rabbit hole of endless comparison articles. Case in point, a Google search for '*best email service providers for authors*' turns up 7,940,000,000 results as of March 2022. That's an enormous amount of data to shuffle through when you have so many other author tasks to tackle.

SO HOW DO YOU CUT THROUGH THE MOUNTAINS OF INFORMATION AND OPINIONS TO FIND THE RIGHT ESP FOR YOU?

While there is no one-size-fits-all approach, one of the best ways to approach the process is to treat it like IT professionals approach software procurement or development projects. One of the key steps in that process is establishing a baseline. This is done by performing a current state analysis, which is basically just a deep dive into how you're doing things now.

To put this into context for an author, you would want to start by assessing where you are in your current author business.

- Are you a new, unpublished author or recently published author with a small or non-existent subscriber list?

- Are you a few years into your business and your list is starting to grow beyond what you can reasonably manage through your current process or ESP?
- Are you a seasoned author with a massive list and need a set of robust tools to help you leverage your subscriber list?

Once you've determined where you are, the next step is to determine where you want to go. This process is similar to the technical needs analysis or business requirement gathering phase of an IT project. This step is all about thinking through how you plan to use your subscriber list.

- When and how often do you plan to reach out to your list?

    - Only occasionally when you have a new release
    - On a predetermined schedule that includes both emails and recurring newsletters
    - Frequently through things like multi-email sequences, ARC teams, or sales campaigns

- How do you plan to grow your list?

    - By a wing, a prayer, and a word of mouth, even if it takes years to build
    - At a moderate pace as you develop a backlist and gain exposure
    - Like a boss, baby! You have big plans that include BookFunnel promos, newsletter swaps, ads, and maybe even a sign twirler if it will get you subscribers

WHY DOES ANY OF THIS EVEN MATTER?

Working out the when, where, and how is a crucial part of the evaluation process because when it comes to choosing an ESP, size really does matter. With most ESPs, the size of your subscriber list and the frequency at which you engage with them has a direct impact on the amount you'll pay. This brings us to the step of the evaluation process where you need to determine your price point. This step is similar to the process of cost estimation and budgeting for an IT project.

Most ESPs offer either a free trial or a low-cost bottom tier plan for managing subscriber lists of less than a thousand unique contacts. As your subscriber list grows or you increase your engagement frequency, the subscription price increases exponentially. If you don't approach your ESP purchase with at least some type of budget in mind, the added cost of scaling your subscriber list can quickly outspend your post release profits.

Most of us are familiar with the old adage, "Time is money," but you'd be surprised how often the need to evaluate time in terms of cost is overlooked during the planning process. When it comes to evaluating time, the first thing you should do is ask yourself the following questions:

- What is my level of technical ability?
- How much work do I want or have the bandwidth to do?

Answering these questions will help you develop a clear picture of the types of tools and features you'll need in an ESP platform. As with most things, the more bells and whistles you want, the more you can expect to pay. One example of this is phone-based tech support. Only a handful of the top-rated ESPs offer this service as part of their free or lower-tier plans. With most ESPs, tech support is only available once you've upgraded to their more advanced, meaning more expensive, tiers.

If you consider yourself tech challenged or loathe the idea of wasting valuable writing time installing and configuring the connection between your website or landing page and your new ESP, you'll either need to pay someone to do it for you or pay out of pocket for a higher-level tier that includes these services. Even something as simple as a lift and shift of your existing list to a new ESP can become complicated and require costly tech support if you're unable or unwilling to tackle the task yourself.

While the steps outlined here are far from all-inclusive, they cover enough basic points of consideration to help you get started with the ESP evaluation process. Once you've narrowed it down to a handful of contenders, you might want to do side-by-side comparisons of features, pricing, and other factors similar to those shown below and to the right to get a high-level view of how your favorites stack up.

Now that you've done your due diligence, the only thing standing between you and one of the most valuable tools in your indie author toolbox is the "subscribe now" button. ■

Jenn Mitchell

Best Free Email Marketing Services Comparison Table

	FREE PLAN	MONTHLY EMAIL SENDS	DAILY EMAIL SENDS	BEST FEATURE	CONS	RATINGS
moosend	Up to 1,000 subscribers (Sign up here)	Unlimited	Unlimited	Rich email templates, Drag-and-drop editor, No Moosend branding in emails	Limited native integrations (Zapier & Piesync available)	
sendinblue	Free for unlimited subscribers	9,000	300	SMS personalization features, Page tracking	Sendinblue logo in emails, dated email template designs	
HubSpot	Up to 2,000 email sends	2,000	No Limit	Free CRM	HubSpot logo in emails, restrictive monthly email sends limit	
mailer lite	Up to 1,000 subscribers	12,000	.	A/B testing options, Embedded sign-up forms	No newsletter templates & live chat support, Mailerlite logo in emails	
mailchimp	Up to 2,000 subscribers	10,000	2,000	Behavioral targeting tools, Facebook & Instagram Ads	Mailchimp logo in emails, lack of proper support (only tutorials and guides in free plan)	
Mailjet	Free for unlimited subscribers	6,000	200	APIs, SMTP Relay, Webhooks	Mailjet logo in emails, no online support, limited segmentation	
SendPulse	Up to 500 subscribers	15,000	No Limit	Resend to non-openers, Heatmaps	No A/B testing, difficult to manage automations	
EmailOctopus	Up to 2,500 subscribers	10,000	.	Easy-to-use Editor, Affiliate marketing friendly	EmailOctopus logo in emails, statistics stored for 30 days only	
BENCHMARK	N/A	250	.	Live engagement reports, Drag-and-drop editor	Email deliverability issues, only basic automation	
CleverReach	Up to 250 subscribers	1,000	.	Reminder emails and autoresponders, Reporting	CleverReach ads in newsletters & signup forms, not great email deliverability	

https://moosend.com/blog/free-email-marketing-services/ collected on 3/24/2022

sendinblue

Solutions ▾   Pricing   Features ▾   Resources ▾   Blog

EN ▾   Log in   **Sign up free**

Pricing plans

All plans come with <u>unlimited contact storage</u>.

POPULAR

Free
Getting started with Sendinblue

$0 /month

Sign up

✓ Unlimited contacts
✓ Up to 300 emails per day
✓ Chat (1 user)

Lite
Perfect for new marketers

$25/month

Monthly email volume:

10K   100K+

10,000 Emails

Sign up

Everything in Free, and:

✓ No daily sending limit
✓ Email support
✓ Lite+ add-on: A/B testing, remove Sendinblue logo, advanced statistics

Calculate your price

Premium
Best solution for marketing pros

$65/month

Monthly email volume:

20K   1000K+

20,000 Emails

Sign up

Everything in Lite+, and:

✓ Marketing Automation
✓ Facebook ads
✓ Landing pages
✓ Multi-user access
✓ Telephone Support

Calculate your price

Enterprise
For marketers who need more

Have more advanced needs?

Get quote

Everything in Premium, and:

✓ Custom volume of emails
✓ Priority sending
✓ 20+ landing pages
✓ Access for 10+ users
✓ SSO (SAML)
✓ Customer success manager
✓ Priority support
✓ <u>And more...</u>

<u>https://kinsta.com/blog/mailchimp-alternatives/</u> collected on 3/24/2022

Subscribers	Emails / month	Monthly cost
1 - 1,000	12,000	Free ❓
1 - 1,000	Unlimited	$ 10
1,001 - 2,500	Unlimited	$ 15
2,501 - 5,000	Unlimited	$ 30
5,001 - 10,000	Unlimited	$ 50

https://kinsta.com/blog/mailchimp-alternatives/ collected on 3/24/2022

PLOTTR: PRO LEVEL UNLOCKED

SNEAK A PEEK AT NEW FEATURES COMING TO THE WRITING SOFTWARE THIS MONTH

With more than ten thousand authors already using Plottr, the story outlining and organizational software, many indie authors already find plenty of value in the platform and its features. A previous article published in May 2021 in *Indie Author Magazine* took a deep dive into potential uses and determined it was a solid tool for a variety of author types.

But good things can always improve, and now the company is hoping the new Plottr Pro, set to be available May 11, will do just that.

"One of the important things for us was to make it as accessible as possible to as many people as possible," says Plottr co-founder Ryan Zee. "In a way, the Pro version is geared towards people who want to be able to use and plot from wherever they are, whether that's online or from a device that can't install a desktop program on it. We also know that people can have difficulty figuring out how to sync files across devices, so we wanted to make that easier for people. On the collaboration front, we know that a lot of authors work with editors or co-authors and collaborators, and we wanted to make that process easier."

The existing Plottr functions include the ability to visually organize stories on Windows, Mac, Android, and iOS; create story and series bibles; use a variety of plot templates; and the option to export files to Microsoft Word and Scrivener.

In addition, Plottr Pro will introduce the following new features:

- Access to Plottr on web, desktop, and mobile
- Online and offline use
- Automatic syncing across all devices
- Collaboration between multiple parties in real time (Note: All parties will require Pro accounts to work in a document simultaneously.)
- Built-in cloud backups
- Improved mobile experience
- Availability on Chromebook

Of course, lists are fine and dandy, but what does any of that mean for those already using Plottr? How do you decide, awesome author that you are, whether you need to look into this new upgrade?

If we're being honest, maybe you don't. Maybe the templates and series bibles are the best bang for your buck. But if you like to work on the same document on your tablet, phone, and laptop at any given time; forget to save your progress periodically; or work with co-authors or collaborators, Plottr Pro might be the way to go.

And while the first release of Plottr Pro will have the additional functionality listed above, even more updates in the works will be rolled out to Pro subscribers in the future at no additional cost. These will include commenting, tracked changes, and editing history—all features MS Word fans are likely already familiar with.

Plottr and Plottr Pro are just two tools to consider when building your author toolbox. As with any tool or program, you must decide if this works for you. The basic Plottr program includes a free fourteen-day trial and subscription rates starting at $25 annually or $99 for a lifetime subscription on a single device. The Pro version will also include annual and lifetime rates, and though annual rates are still being finalized, Zee says lifetime subscriptions will be offered for $297. More information about Plottr Pro is available on the Plottr YouTube channel, the Plottr email list, and its website, http://plottr.com. ◼

Bre Lockhart

If you'd like to learn more about technology for authors, including Plottr, visit https://IndieAuthorTools.com, and stay tuned for more information on Indie Author Magazine's inaugural Author Tech Summit happening later this year!

Tech Tools

Courtesy of IndieAuthorTools.com
Got a tool you love and want to share with us?
Submit a tool at IndieAuthorTools.com

BOOK-FUNNEL

BookFunnel simplifies getting your reader magnet onto your email subscriber's preferred e-reading device while lifting the technical delivery hassles from you. This author service specializes in ebook and audio distribution.
https://bookfunnel.com/

KINGSUMO

When done correctly, a giveaway can help you build an email list with quality subscribers and increase your book sales. KingSumo is an easy-to-use platform that helps you create viral giveaways quickly. Just open the tool, write a few lines about your giveaway, and enter the number of winners.
https://appsumo.8odi.net/5b17go

LOOM

Thinking about creating a video to use as a reader magnet? A free screen-capture tool like Loom makes a handy item for your toolkit. In addition to easy video creation, Loom provides tools to monitor the performance of your cookie.
https://www.loom.com/

HOLLY DARLING HQ

Holly Darling HQ is a boutique marketing agency run by a self-published author who is an email marketing consultant. Darling says her mission is to teach writers how to use emails to increase their sales and cultivate loyal fan bases. You'll find free resources and tips, along with her paid courses, on the website.
https://hollydarlinghq.com/

SUBSCRIBER REVIVER CHALLENGE

Subscriber Reviver is a 15-day challenge designed to help you re-engage your email audience. The event is based on Yara Golden's StorySelling method. "You don't own a list, you have the privilege of having an audience — made up of people who've chosen to pay attention to you," Golden says. "Entertain them, educate them, treat them with respect, and [your] offers will become an easy yes."
https://subscriberreviver.com/

A True 'Slice of Life' Story

THE SECRETS TO MAKING MEMOIRS THAT MEAN SOMETHING

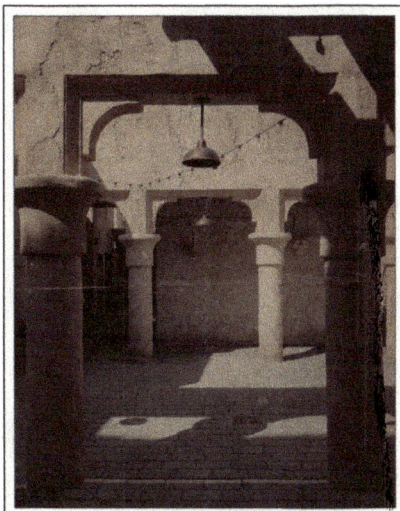

In his essay titled "The Narrative Idea," David Halberstam has a simple piece of advice for writers who want to succeed at their craft: "The idea is vital."

His words, published in 2007 in the book *Telling True Stories*, were directed toward narrative journalists, but they apply to some extent across every genre, whether fiction or nonfiction. "Telling a good story demands a great conception, a great idea for why the story works—for what it is and how it connects to the human condition," he wrote.

For memoirists especially, that last bit seems intuitive. Of course, the story is connected to the human condition, right? It's the author's own lived experience, after all.

But for a genre that's grounded solidly in reality, its structure is not always so straightforward. And in these stories, narrowing down a central message from all the thoughts and emotions on the page is just one of the ways authors can start to improve their narratives so that they make a stronger impact on readers.

WHAT MAKES A MEMOIR?

Running the gamut from ordinary conversations to life-changing revelations, memoirs frequently climb to the top of nonfiction bestseller lists. In recent years, they seem to be growing in popularity among writers too, especially within the independent publishing world, according to a 2019 Publisher's Weekly article (https://publishersweekly.com). Reaching a

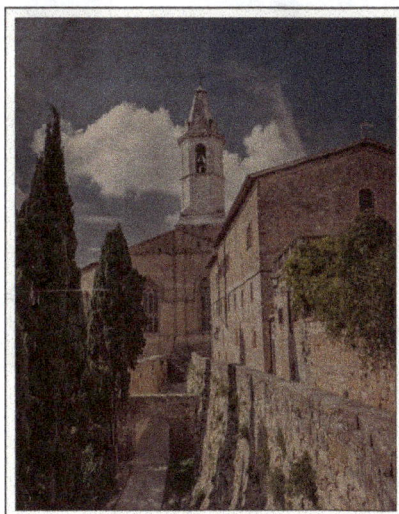

deal with a publishing agent is notoriously difficult, but memoirists who don't have an already solid reader base or who lack a unique story to tell may struggle even more to find representation in the traditional publishing world. Couple that with the many memoirists who write more for their own catharsis than for profits, and it's no surprise authors would turn to small independent presses or self-publishing to distribute their books.

Still, none of that is to imply writing creative nonfiction will automatically create a bestseller or even that it will be easy.

"A successful essay takes [the] reader on a thinking journey," writes Julija Šukys, associate professor of English at the University of Missouri. The same is true of memoir—or any creative nonfiction genre, for that matter. "It moves between the small and the big. It observes details of ordinary life and also thinks about the biggest human questions."

Memoirs shouldn't contain an author's every interaction or memory, according to Publisher's Weekly—think "slice of life," even if the rough drafts sometimes start to feel like the whole pie.

They don't all need to be ground-breaking tales either, Šukys writes. "For me, the question lies less in whether the experiences are worth telling but whether a writer has something to say. What questions is the writer grappling with? What insights does she bring? Many writers offer startling insights about small and ordinary life experiences."

So how do you decide what makes it into the final version?

According to "Writing Memoir and Writing for Therapy," a craft essay by creative nonfiction author Tara DaPra, you let it sit. It can take time to

parse out the narrative you're shaping, especially if the story is one you're still living. "When you return to revisit the work, you can try to make some sense of the raw material," according to DaPra. In the process, you will find which details can stay in the manuscript and which deserve to be cut.

PERFECTING THE CRAFT

Finding the underlying story in your manuscript might be the first hurdle memoirists face, but it is far from the only one. Since real life rarely follows an organized narrative structure, authors must also decide how to build one from the pieces they've been given.

"Pacing is key," Šukys writes, as it is with any genre in order to build tension. So is maintaining your readers' trust, both in your ability to resolve the story and in its truthfulness.

It's a more nuanced promise than it sounds. Although some nonfiction genres—such as narrative journalism or academic text—hold a strict definition when it comes to the truth, memoirs can be more flexible. For one, human memory is naturally faulty, according to The Atlantic (https://theatlantic.com), so authors writing about events just as they remember them will inevitably be inaccurate. And for another, small edits or omissions, such as the combination of two people into one "character," have long been accepted by some readers in order to tell a better story or provide anonymity.

So how can authors know where to take liberties in their memoir?

Ultimately, the decision is up to them, though journalist Roy Peter Clark's "The Line Between Fact and Fiction" offers two principles to attempt to make the distinction more clear: Do not add anything, and do not deceive. Author and memoir coach Marion Roach Smith expanded on the idea further in an <u>interview with The Creative Penn podcast</u> (https://thecreativepenn.com): "Show us the real. Don't make yourself out to be something you never were. We can smell that a mile away, and we can smell it in dialogue more than anything else."

As for altering names in your work, the rules surprisingly can still be built on a case-by-case basis. "CNF [creative nonfiction] writers write from life. It's impossible to ask every person you meet if you can write about them," Šukys writes. Although she chooses to reach out to people she names in her work, she also admits that it can be easier and more ethical to change names for those characters who aren't as essential to the story. And if you're dealing with more legally controversial topics? According to Šukys: "The process can be more adversarial and litigious. In this case, writers should take legal advice."

CORNERING THE MARKET

With all the work that goes into introspection, research, and story craft, memoirs and creative nonfiction can seem easier to edit than write—at least in the sense that the process is much the same as that of fiction writers. One of the largest challenges authors might face is in critiquing their own work. It is, after all, their life story on the page. In these situations, Šukys makes two suggestions. The first, from her own editing process, is to read the draft aloud. "I'm a big believer in editing through the ear. We stop seeing errors, repetitions, and sloppy language after a time, so the best thing to do is read your book or essay aloud or have your computer read it to you."

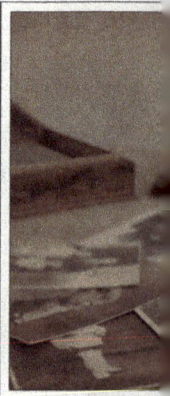

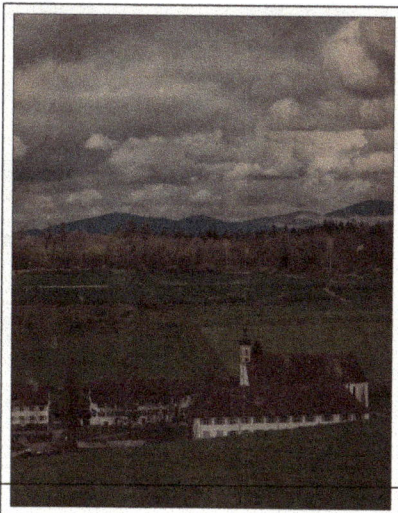

Secondly, she encourages authors to find a community among other authors. Visit conferences, writer groups, and even local libraries—"they are the greatest resource a budding writer could ask for," she writes. DaPra gives the same advice in her essay, offering that writers can share their work with others when sorting through a draft to help tease out any narrative threads worth developing.

Pro Tip: Typically, memoirs run between eighty thousand and one-hundred thousand words in length or about the same as general fiction novels, according to ProWritingAid.

And what about when the book is done? In the case of marketing, as in the revision process, the learning curve isn't quite as steep from fiction to nonfiction. Most writing and self-publishing resources recommend identifying a target audience and building a presence online and through social media—the same tips often recommended to authors in other genres. In your messaging, Roach Smith said, focus on the universal lessons in your story rather than on the story itself, and don't be afraid to try something new and unique to connect with your readers.

Ultimately, memoir is "an outsider art," according to Publisher's Weekly, filled by authors who are willing to shirk trends and tropes within an industry to tell true stories. If you pay attention to craft, narrative, and the "great idea" at the center of it all, it doesn't matter whether the story you choose to tell is commonplace. Some of the most beloved pieces of creative nonfiction are.

What matters most are the truths about yourself you learn in the process. ■

Nicole Schroeder

Podcasts We Love

Inbox Besties Podcast
Kate Doster brings you practical advice and tips for growing your email list in her show. She believes "email marketing can be fun and profitable when you treat people like people and let your personality shine through."
https://www.katedoster.com/inbox-besties/

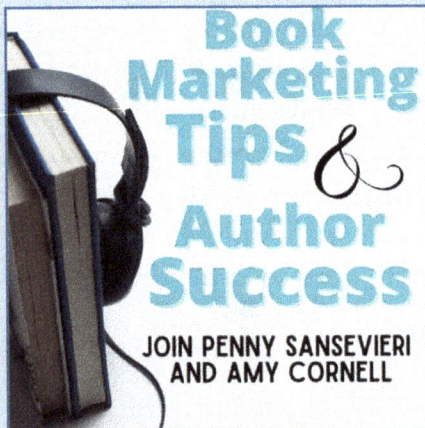

Book Marketing Tips and Author Success
If your book marketing plan needs work, check out Penny Sansevieri and Amy Cornell's show. Their podcast is long on new ideas and easy-to-implement book marketing strategies. It's designed to help self-published and traditionally published authors at any career level grow their platform.
https://podcasts.apple.com/us/podcast/book-marketing-tips-and-author-success-podcast/id1500195014

How Writers Write
Brian Murphy interviews successful writers "to decode their tips, routines, and motivations for producing best-sellers" on the How Writers Write show. Recent listeners have been privy to an insider's glimpse into the lives of J.A. Jance, Maurice Ruffin, and Fiona Davis.
https://podcasts.apple.com/us/podcast/how-writers-write-by-happywriter/id1484859401

It's a Cinch: The Fact and Fiction of Corsets

Valerie Steel begins her study *The Corset: A Cultural History* claiming, "The corset is probably the most controversial garment in the entire history of fashion." Considering its reputation as oppressive, torturous, and downright dangerous, it's hard to argue.

High time, then, we unknotted fact from fiction when it comes to this complex garment.

As with any facet of fiction and historical research, it's for you to decide your level of detail and accuracy and consider your audience. Does it matter if you use the word "corset" in your seventeenth-century-inspired Fantasy story (strictly speaking, the era-appropriate term would be "stays")? What about your painstakingly researched Historical Fiction set in the court of Louis XIV?

WHAT IS A CORSET?

Broadly speaking, a corset is a stiffened, tightly fitted garment that supports the torso. Shapes fluctuated with fashionable silhouettes, but they were worn almost ubiquitously by women of all kinds in

European-influenced cultures from the sixteenth until the twentieth centuries.

It's important to understand the stays worn by your Elizabethan heroine were very different from the corset her many-times-great-granddaughter wore three hundred years later. This is an area where research is your friend, but beware of sensationalized reports (and check the myth-busting section below). The historical costuming community is a great resource.

MYTH VERSUS REALITY

Many, *many* myths surround corsets, so we'll tackle a few of the most common beliefs and see if any stand up to closer scrutiny.

First, no, women in the Victorian era almost certainly didn't have ribs removed to achieve a smaller waist. No documented evidence supports this, and considering the huge risks of infection at the time, any elective surgery was a bad idea, never mind one as major as rib removal.

Yes, corsets are capable of moving the organs. So too is yoga, pregnancy, or simply eating a large meal. Some evidence shows that regular corset-wearing, especially from a young age, might affect the shape of the ribcage; however, many modern women develop dents in their rib cages and/or shoulders from wearing bras.

"Can you breathe in that?" Yes, women of the nineteenth century were just as fond of oxygen as those in the twenty-first century. A properly fitting corset only reduces the waist, so it shifts the wearer's breathing higher in their chest, giving that "heaving bosom" effect.

"All Victorian women tightlaced!" This is a myth. Tightlacing (where the waist is reduced by several inches) is the most common corset trope; however, it wasn't the norm. The small waists seen in photographs from the era were often achieved using early photo manipulation or the contrast of large skirts, sleeves, or bust/hip padding against a lightly cinched waist.

"You can't put a corset on without at least one maid!" This is another myth. In the cultures/eras discussed, almost all women wore corsets/stays, even the very poor. The split busk—the steel closure still seen at the front of modern corsets—was introduced in the mid-nineteenth century and made it easier to put on a corset unaided. Searching "how to put on a corset by yourself" yields various videos that show the process.

"Women couldn't do anything wearing corsets!" This is yet another myth. "All women" above includes maids and other workers. Certain styles were even developed to allow women to more easily ride horses or bicycles and take part in sports, such as tennis and mountain climbing. Videos show modern corset-wearers weightlifting and sword fighting; they are not straight jackets.

"Women hated corsets," and "my heroine refuses to wear one!" Like any historical issue, attitudes toward corsets were not homogenous. Steele's book is an excellent study of the subject. Remember, in that era, a woman was considered undressed and even indecent without a corset. Any heroine who showed up at an 1880s ball uncorseted would be the talk of the town for all the wrong reasons.

Finally, as a remedy to their "dangerous" reputation, we'll end on the reports of women saved by their corsets, such as the case of Mary Sarah Phillips (see Margaret Drinkall's *19th Century Barnsley Murders*) whose steel-boned corset broke her attacker's blade when he stabbed her. Admittedly, corsets weren't designed for this purpose, and it's a matter of luck that the knife hit a steel bone, but isn't fiction so often about the fortunate misses and the gunshots that hit the lucky cigar case? ▪

Clare Sager

THE WOMEN OF GAMELIT

MAKING THEIR MARK ON THE FRONTLINES OF A MALE-DOMINATED GENRE

According to a 2021 article in Forbes, women accounted for nearly 41 percent of the gamer population in the United States and up to 45 percent in Asia, which also sees 48 percent of the world's total video game revenue.

While reader demographics are almost impossible to evaluate—the numbers simply aren't readily available—a quick review of five well-known US LitRPG publishers shows only about 13 percent of their named authors use she/her pronouns in their bios. A cursory glance at a few popular podcasts about these genres revealed only two interviewees who were women—both narrators, not authors—and a lengthy list of interviewed men. And if you spend any time in the various LitRPG author and reader groups on Facebook, it's apparent that the demographics skew more toward males.

Why the possible disconnect between women who enjoy video games and women who write in video game worlds? Hard to say, but when it comes to that 13 percent of female authors, the powerful stories they're writing are helping women stake a claim in subgenres already experiencing huge growth within the indie author industry.

GENRE SANDBOX

Have you ever seen the movies *Jumanji* or *Ready Player One* or read the books they're based on? What about the more recent original movie *Free Guy*? Yep, those are all some flavor of GameLit.

Essentially, GameLit and its associated subgenres are stories with game elements woven in. In LitRPG, a genre connected to GameLit, more statistics and rules might come into play, but even under that heading, the stories can follow many paths.

According to all the authors we interviewed, following the reader's expectations for the subgenre you've chosen matters. "I would caution … that if your game does not have stat boxes or if it's only GameLit adjacent, do not market it as such," GameLit author Jay Boyce says. "For the love of all that is holy, do not say it's a LitRPG/GameLit book. People will get angry. Pick the right one and stick to it, and make sure your book actually has those elements. There is nothing worse than the bait and switch."

THE FEMALE PROTAGONIST

In other modern fantasy genres, such as Urban Fantasy, you'll find no shortage of female main characters. GameLit, however, appears to be an outlier with that trend, author Jess Mountifield says. "It's tough to get all the readers to take a chance on a female-led book in the genre. It's still my preferred choice, but it has meant that sometimes I've gone with a male lead."

The authors interviewed all seemed to agree that lead character diversity is a concern. "What it needs more of is acceptance that not all people are like you—'you' as in 'everyone is different.' Sometimes the genre feels a little tunnel visioned in what sort of people the MC [main character] and surrounding entourage can be. I would love to see more female MCs, but most female authors I know have even steered away from writing them and have chosen to focus on male MCs instead," says author K.T. Hanna.

A lack of female leads seems to correlate with the lack of female authors. "Honestly, I want more female perspectives," Boyce says. "The genre is heavily male-dominated right now. I know there are so many female gamers out there, so many female authors. I've even found several lately that I didn't know were writing in the genre because they wrote books and published them in various places without taking advantage and becoming part of the pre-built communities."

In fact, statements like, "It's hard, but … something I love doing" and "To be honest, it's been a little

tough," were common when asked about what it's like being a female author in the GameLit subgenres.

"Sadly, most guys don't like [reading about] girls in the genre," author Dawn Chapman says.

Mountifield offered her own perspective. "There are some subgenres that can make it feel like this is a genre that doesn't respect women much, and there's always a male writer in every genre who doesn't respect women. But there are also some great guys in the genre who want us to be here and want women to both read and write this."

LIGHT AT THE END OF THE DUNGEON

Without glazing over the above concerns, the authors interviewed were quick to point out some of the shining moments of the genre as well.

As Chapman puts it, "We really are a very close knit community, and that matters. Authors and fans are all very protective."

And that point is incredibly evident when you visit GameLit-heavy spaces like Discord servers, Reddit threads, and Facebook groups. These authors know one another; they collaborate. On serialized platforms like Royal Road and places like Patreon, they are often huge fans of their peers. These authors champion the works and successes of their communities.

Authors also have the opportunity to find immense satisfaction writing in such an interesting and evolving genre. "One of my favorite things as an author is actually the surprising amount of parents I get messaging me because they were able to use my books to connect and read with their teenagers. They're always very excited to find a book that they can share," Boyce says.

PORTAL TO THE FUTURE

Numerous stories of connections have been forged between parties because of a shared love of literature, but a genre that could potentially transcend generational gaps in new ways is noteworthy. The genre is evolving and expanding at a breakneck pace, possibly even more so.

Hanna was optimistic the same genre evolution might occur on the reader's side. "The genre has grown so much since I started writing in it. I'd love to see people who aren't necessarily gamers fall in love with it too, but that might be too much to ask. But it would be nice if every single gamer found it and devoured it. After all—writing is what we do. It's nice if it can pay the bills."

Boyce also added her take on what the genre might see in the future. "I honestly think this is only the start. The genre as we know it only started gaining traction a little over five years ago. Gaming is such a normal part of people's lives now, and books allow you to encapsulate large stretches of gaming without having to actually go and grind for months …. The genre is here to stay, and it's only going to get bigger from here on out."

With five-figure Facebook reader groups and an extremely participatory and integrated customer base, the genre indeed appears to be here to stay.

Many thanks to Dawn Chapman, Jay Boyce, Jess Mountifield, and KT Hanna for their assistance with this article. For more information about each, please visit their Amazon author pages or website listed below. ■

Bre Lockhart

With thanks to:

Dawn Chapman, author of *Puatera Online*: https://dawn-chapmanauthor.com

Jay Boyce, author of the *A Touch of Power* series: https://jayboyce.com/

Jess Mountifield (who also writes as Talia Beckett), author of the *Fringe Colonies* Saga: https://jessmountifield.co.uk

KT Hanna, author of the *Somnia Online* series: https://kthanna.com

WRITING WITH CHRONIC ILLNESS: CREATIVE WAYS TO KEEP CREATING

Since March 2020, the COVID-19 pandemic has put a spotlight on chronic illnesses. Early estimates indicate anywhere from 5 to 80 percent of people experience lasting symptoms after contracting COVID-19, according to the Centers for Disease Control and Prevention (https://cdc.gov). They join the approximately 51.8 percent of people in the US who live with a chronic condition already, according to the 2018 National Health Institute Survey.

H. E. Casson at the Spoonie Authors Network (https://spoonieauthorsnetwork.com) writes to those adjusting to life with such a diagnosis, "You're about to become a gatherer" of useful tools. There's no be-all, end-all answer to managing life with a chronic illness, they write, and some days, it will inevitably mean letting your body dictate the schedule.

But in the long run, changing the way you think about writing might be key to better accommodating your health while keeping your author's heart happy.

WRITING IN OTHER MEDIUMS IS STILL WRITING

On days that are particularly painful or taxing, words don't have to come from a keyboard while sitting at a desk. Write on your phone or tablet while lying in bed, or find a notebook if screens are bothersome.

Dictation is another option, and though several programs are available at a cost, most word processors have rudimentary versions built in for free. Or opt for an even simpler route: Record your words as a voice memo for you, a friend, or your computer to transcribe later.

DON'T TACKLE EVERYTHING AT ONCE

An author's to-do list is ever-growing. That doesn't mean you have to check everything off at the same time. Your work will still be there tomorrow, and completing only what you have the energy for rather than pushing yourself will help keep you from burning out. Cait Gordon, also at the Spoonie Authors Network, suggests creating a fatigue budget to ensure you have adequate time to rest without feeling as if you're neglecting your responsibilities.

REDEFINE PRODUCTIVITY

You don't need to write a set number of words in a day to call yourself an author. Be realistic when setting goals, and remember that even small word counts add up over time—check out the Word Crawl for the Motivationally Challenged for proof. And give yourself grace on days your health takes precedence over your manuscript. The Twitter account @CountsAsWriting might sum it up best: "Hey. You're doing your best. It counts." ■

Nicole Schroeder

Four R's to Find Your essential Work . . . Instead of Rabbit Holes!

You've heard people talk about creating a minimum viable product. How about a minimum viable process? Your time and energy are valuable—and limited—resources. How much work do you really need to create and market your books? Use these 4 R's to find the essential work.

Risk—Send it off. Email it to your beta reader or editor or hit publish. Test the edges of your process to see how much is necessary. Fear is an excellent tool for finding new risks that might matter. Gently now, test one scary thing at a time. If it works, congratulations. If it doesn't, you can take it off your to-do list. And test something else.

Restlessness—Are you nervous about a scene or a strategy? Restlessness is a cue that you are facing a worthwhile risk. Do you keep finding yourself on social media without a plan? Try moving physically from one writing spot to another. A long walk could also give you the answers you need. Try writing out your questions as clearly as possible before you go. As Anne Janzer writes: "Technology is most tempting when the work is difficult."

Recycle—Review your plan (instead of email or social media) or review your draft from the day before. It's more restful than email, social media, sales tracking or [insert favorite crutch activity here]. It grounds you in your own agenda, instead of letting your writing career be blown by every wind on social media.

Relinquish—Now that you've narrowed down your work, let the rest go. Anxiety about external goals powers up your internal critic, so you can't do your best work. Trust is a doorway into the low-friction flow state, the sweet spot of creativity.

Refining your creative process with **Risk, Restlessness, Recycle,** and **Relinquish** gives you actionable knowledge, so you can find ways to rest. Now that you've stabilized your process, you can trust it. ◼

Laurel Decher

RESOURCES

The Writer's Process: Getting Your Brain in Gear by Anne H. Janzer

FROM THE STACKS

Courtesy of IndieAuthorTools.com
Got a book you love and want to share with us?
Submit a book at IndieAuthorTools.com

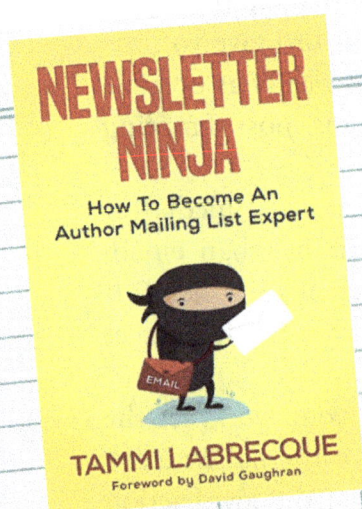

Newsletter Ninja: How to Become an Author Mailing List Expert
Audiobook available

Discover new ways to think about your email list with Newsletter Ninja: How to Become an Author Mailing List Expert. This book is "designed to teach you how to build and maintain a strongly engaged email list – one full of actual fans willing to pay for the books you write, rather than free-seekers who will forget your name and never open your emails."

https://www.amazon.com/Newsletter-Ninja-Become-Author-Mailing-ebook/dp/B07C6J8HP9/?tag=indieauthortools-20

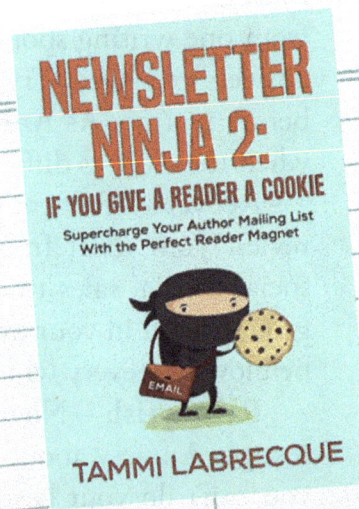

Newsletter Ninja 2: If You Give a Reader a Cookie: Supercharge Your Author Mailing List With the Perfect Reader Magnet

Whether you're new to the concept of cookies (aka reader magnets) or need to revamp the ones you have, Newsletter Ninja 2 has you covered. Learn the two types of cookies, the dos and don'ts for both, and the strategies to consider. This little gem is chock-full of actionable ideas and author Tammi Labrecque's signature humor.

https://www.amazon.com/Newsletter-Ninja-Supercharge-Mailing-Perfect-ebook/dp/B09L9KPKY9/?tag=indieauthortools-20

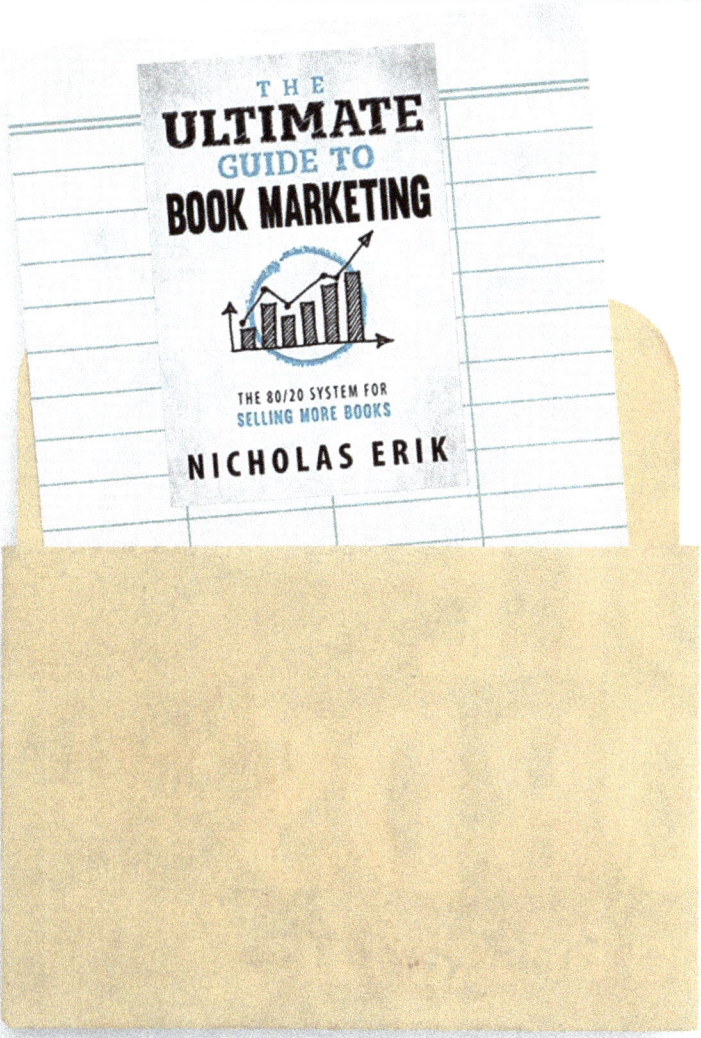

The Ultimate Guide to Book Marketing: The 80/20 System for Selling More Books

Nicholas Erik covers book marketing from strategy to blurbs to newsletters, complete with exercises created to help you implement what you learn. Topics include: how to build your newsletter, how to cultivate newsletter engagement, how to get an effective cover, how to launch your book, and how retailers help you sell more books.

https://www.amazon.com/Ultimate-Guide-Book-Marketing-Selling/dp/B08C453YDN/?tag=indieauthortools-20

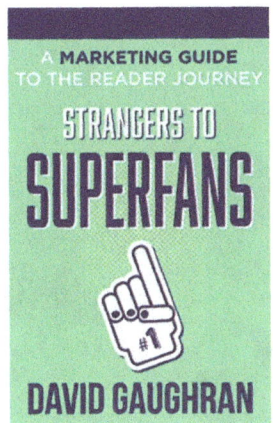

Strangers To Superfans: A Marketing Guide to The Reader Journey

Audiobook available

In this book, David Gaughran lays out the journey your "Ideal Readers" take in a transformation from strangers to your superfans. You will learn to optimize each stage of the journey to increase conversion and boost sales by making the process more frictionless.

https://www.amazon.com/dp/B0798PH9QT/?tag=indieauthortools-20

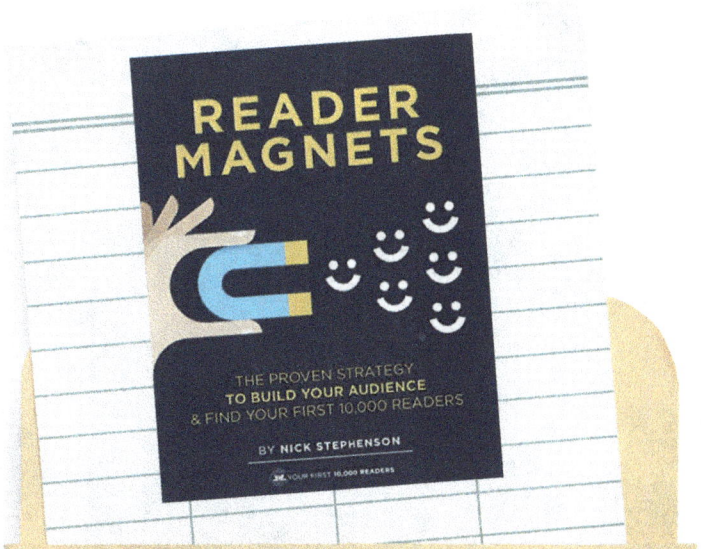

Reader Magnets: Build Your Author Platform and Sell More Books on Kindle (2022 Edition)

Looking for "clear instructions and zero fluff" to help you create your author platform? In Nick Stephenson's 2022 edition of Reader Magnets, he discusses the importance of reader magnets and how to use them to build your email subscriber list. A sample email sequence is provided.

https://www.amazon.com/Reader-Magnets-Platform-Marketing-Authors-ebook/dp/B00PCKIJ4C/?tag=indieauthortools-20

INDIE AUTHOR
NEWS & EVENTS

For the latest on news and events pertinent to the indie author community, please check out our interactive calendar here:

Got news or events to share with the Indie Author Community? Let us know at news@indieauthormagazine.com.

In This Issue

Executive Team

Chelle Honiker, Publisher

As the publisher of Indie Author Magazine, Chelle Honiker brings nearly three decades of startup, technology, training, and executive leadership experience to the role. She's a serial entrepreneur, founding and selling multiple successful companies including a training development company, travel agency, website design and hosting firm, a digital marketing consultancy, and a wedding planning firm. She's organized and curated multiple TEDx events and hired to assist other nonprofit organizations as a fractional executive, including The Travel Institute and The Freelance Association.

As a writer, speaker, and trainer she believes in the power of words and their ability to heal, inspire, incite, and motivate. Her greatest inspiration is her daughters, Kelsea and Cathryn, who tolerate her tendency to run away from home to play with her friends around the world for months at a time. It's said she could run a small country with just the contents of her backpack.

Alice Briggs, Creative Director

As the creative director of Indie Author Magazine, Alice Briggs utilizes her more than three decades of artistic exploration and expression, business startup adventures, and leadership skills. A serial entrepreneur, she has started several successful businesses. She brings her experience in creative direction, magazine layout and design, and graphic design in and outside of the indie author community to her role.

With a masters of science in Occupational Therapy, she has a broad skill set and uses it to assist others in achieving their desired goals. As a writer, teacher, healer, and artist, she loves to see people accomplish all they desire. She's excited to see how IAM will encourage many authors to succeed in whatever way they choose. She hopes to meet many of you in various places around the world once her passport is back in use.

Writers

Angela Archer

Having worked as a mental health nurse for many years, Angela combines her love of words with her love of human psychology to work as a copywriter in the UK. She independently published a novella and novel in 2020 and is currently fending off the lure of shiny new novel ideas to complete the second book in her sci-fi series.

When she's not tinkering with words, she's usually drinking tea, playing the saxophone (badly), or being mum and wife to her husband and two boys.

Bradley Charbonneau

Bradley Charbonneau wanted to be a writer. Trouble was, he didn't write. A friend was running a "Monthly Experiment" (no coffee for a month, wake up at 5 AM, etc.) and created one where everyone had to write every single day for 30 days. Bradley took the challenge. "Hmm, that wasn't so bad." Then he kept going. 100 days. 365. 1,000. 2,808 days and 31 books later and he found out it's simple. Not necessarily easy, but simple. #write #everysingleday

Laurel Decher

There might be no frigate like a book, but publishing can feel like a voyage on the H.M.S. Surprise. There's always a twist and there's never a moment to lose.

Laurel's mission is to help you make the most of today's opportunities. She's a strategic problem-solver, tool collector, and co-inventor of the "you never know" theory of publishing.

As an epidemiologist, she studied factors that help babies and toddlers thrive. Now she writes books for children ages nine to twelve about finding more magic in life. She's a member of the Society for Children's Book Writers and Illustrators (SCBWI), has various advanced degrees, and a tendency to smuggle vegetables into storylines.

Gill Fernley

Gill Fernley writes fiction in several genres under different pen names, but what all of them have in common is humour and romance, because she can't resist a happy ending or a good laugh. She's also a freelance content writer and has been running her own business since 2013. Before that, she was a technical author and documentation manager for an engineering company and can describe to you more than you'd ever wish to know about airflow and filtration in downflow booths. Still awake? Wow, that's a first! Anyway, that experience taught her how to explain complex things in straightforward language and she hopes it will come in handy for writing articles for IAM. Outside of writing, she's a cake decorator, expert shoe hoarder, and is fluent in English, dry humour and procrastibaking.

Chrishaun Keller-Hanna

Chrishaun Keller-Hanna is an award-winning journalist, teacher, technical writer, and fiction author that lives for explaining difficult concepts in a way that non-technical readers can understand.

She spent twenty years teaching literacy and composition to a variety of students from kindergarten to college level and writing technical documentation for several tech companies in the Austin area. At the age of forty-three, she decided to write fiction and has published over thirty titles so far with plans to extend out to comics and board games.

When she's not writing, she's traveling, playing video games, or watching movies. When she's not doing THAT, she's talking about them with her husband and grown daughters.

Bre Lockhart

Armed with a degree in Communications and Public Relations, Bre Lockhart survived more than a decade in the corporate America trenches before jumping headfirst into writing urban fantasy and sci-fi, followed later by mystery under a second pen name. She's also one-third of a fiction editing team who probably enjoy their jobs a bit too much most days. As an experienced extrovert, Bre uses her questionable humor and red—sometimes other colors, too—glasses at writer conferences to draw unsuspecting introverts into her bubble of conversation; no one is safe. On her days off, you can find Bre camping and traveling with her family or organizing an expansive collection of lipstick at her home in Tulsa, Oklahoma.

Merri Maywether

Merri Maywether lives with her husband in rural Montana. You can find her in the town's only coffee house listening to three generations of Montanans share their stories. Otherwise, she's in the classroom or the school library, inspiring the next generation's writers.

Jenn Mitchell

Jenn Mitchell writes Urban Fantasy and Weird West, as well as culinary cozy mysteries under the pen name, J Lee Mitchell. She writes, cooks, and gardens in the heart of South Central Pennsylvania's Amish Country. When she's not doing these things, she dreams of training llama riding ninjas.

She enjoys traveling, quilting, hoarding cookbooks, Sanntangling, and spending time with the World's most patient and loving significant other.

Susan Odev

Susan has banked over three decades of work experience in the fields of personal and organizational development, being a freelance corporate trainer and consultant alongside holding down "real" jobs for over twenty-five years. Specializing in entrepreneurial mindsets, she has written several non-fiction business books, once gaining a coveted Amazon #1 best seller tag in business and entrepreneurship, an accolade she now strives to emulate with her fiction.

Currently working on her fifth novel, under a top secret pen name, the craft and marketing aspects of being a successful indie author equally fascinate and terrify her.

A lover of history with a criminal record collection, Susan lives in a retro orange and avocado world. Once described by a colleague as being an "onion," Susan has many layers, as have ogres (according to Shrek). She would like to think this makes her cool, her teenage children just think she's embarrassing.

Clare Sager

Holding two degrees in creative writing, Clare Sager is an author of steamy Romantic Fantasy and Fantasy Romance, as well as an editor and outline coach. She's based in Nottingham, UK, where she collects fountain pens, lifts weights, and will fight anyone who dares question the place of romance in fantasy stories (or at least give them a stern talking to). She likes cats, coffee, and speaks fluent sarcasm.

Nicole Schroeder

Nicole is a storyteller at heart. A journalist, author, and editor from Columbia, Missouri, she delights in any opportunity to shape her own stories or help others do the same. Graduating with a bachelor's degree from the Missouri School of Journalism and minors in English and Spanish, she's worked as a copyeditor for a small-town newspaper and as an editor for a local arts and culture magazine. Her creative writing has been published in national literary magazines, and she's helped edit numerous fiction and nonfiction books, including a Holocaust survivor's memoir, alongside international independent publishers. When she's not at her writing desk, Nicole is usually in the saddle, cuddling her guinea pigs, or spending time with family. She loves any excuse to talk about Marvel movies and considers National Novel Writing Month its own holiday.

Are you our next
Featured Author?

Tell us your story!

writelink.to/featured

www.ingramcontent.com/pod-product-compliance
Lightning Source LLC
Chambersburg PA
CBHW080425030426
42335CB00020B/2597